KENT STATE UNIVERSITY LIBRARY, KENT, OHIO

Notes for a

Late-Blooming Martyr

Akron Series in Poetry

Akron Series in Poetry

Elton Glaser, Editor

Barry Seiler, *The Waters of Forgetting*

Raeburn Miller, *The Comma After Love: Selected Poems of Raeburn Miller*

William Greenway, *How the Dead Bury the Dead*

Jon Davis, *Scrimmage of Appetite*

Anita Feng, *Internal Strategies*

Susan Yuzna, *Her Slender Dress*

Raeburn Miller, *The Collected Poems of Raeburn Miller*

Clare Rossini, *Winter Morning with Crow*

Barry Seiler, *Black Leaf*

William Greenway, *Simmer Dim*

Jeanne E. Clark, *Ohio Blue Tips*

Beckian Fritz Goldberg, *Never Be the Horse*

Marlys West, *Notes for a Late-Blooming Martyr*

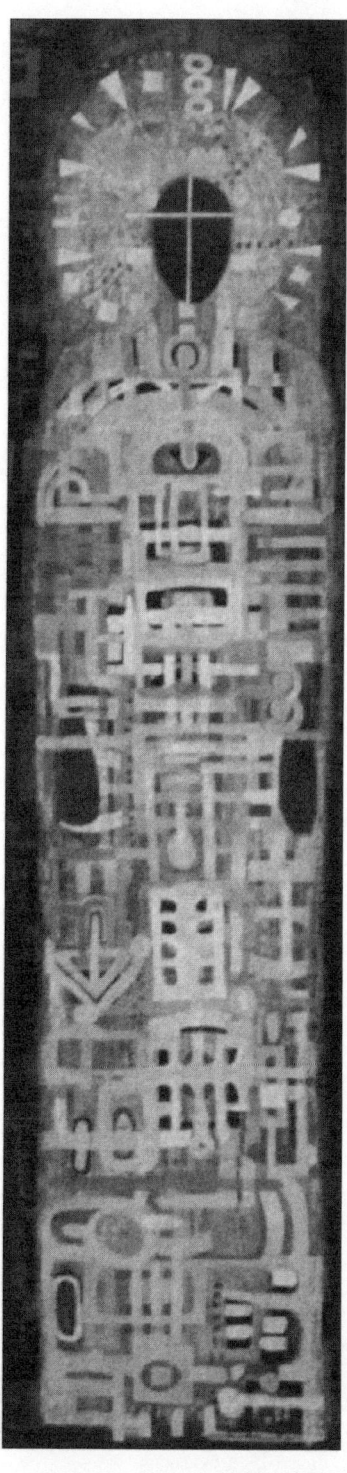

Notes for a Late-Blooming Martyr

Poems by
Marlys West

The University of
Akron Press
Akron, Ohio

© 1999 by Marlys West
All Rights Reserved.

Acknowledgments: Many thanks to Elton Glaser, James A. Michener, and the editors of the following periodicals in whose pages these poems first appeared—*Austin Chronicle:* "Silky Turnpike"; *The Berkeley Poetry Review:* "Any Small Cake or Cookie," "Auntie Star-of-the-Weekend," "Il Fortuna"; *Black Warrior Review:* "Edward"; *Borderlands: Texas Poetry Review:* "Details from the Southeast Quadrant"; *Laurel Review:* "All of a Tin Stove without Heat," "Flor de Tabacos," "You Big Monster You"; *Mississippi Mud:* "Palimpsest of Barefoot Doctors"; *Mississippi Review:* "Is He Floating?"; *This Year's Supper:* "Filters out Twigs and Sticks," "Beautiful Women Are Easy on the Eye"; *Willow Review:* "On Refusing Poison."

Thanks to the Jack S. Blanton Museum of Art, The University of Texas at Austin, for permission to use Margo Hoff's "Color Saints" on the cover. Gift of Mari and James A. Michener, 1968; photo credit to George Holmes.

All inquiries and permissions requests should be addressed to the Publisher, The University of Akron Press, 374B Bierce Library, Akron, Ohio 44325-1703.

LIBRARY OF CONGRESS CATALOGING-IN-PUBLICATION DATA
West, Marlys, 1966–
    Notes for a late-blooming martyr / Marlys West. — 1st ed.
      p. cm. — (Akron series in poetry)
    ISBN 1-884836-55-0 (alk. paper). — ISBN 1-884836-56-9
(pbk. : alk. paper)
    I. Title. II. Series.
PS3573.E82435N68   1999
811'.54—dc21   99-31368
                                                        CIP

Manufactured in the United States of America

The paper used in this publication meets the minumum requirements of American National Standard for Information Sciences—Permanence of Paper for Printed Library Materials, ANSI Z39.48-1984. ∞

First Edition

For Jennifer,
Jonathan, and
Matthew

Contents

ONE

Silky Turnpike	3
Beautiful Women Are Easy on the Eye	5
Living in and alongside Prowlers	6
Loveladies, New Jersey	8
Floating like Plums	9
Arms on Fire	11
The President-Maker	13
Trawl Line, Trawl Line, Sugarplum	15

TWO

Tea-Stained, Vermilion	19
Filters out Twigs and Sticks	21
Plunge	23
The New Plutonium	25
Notes for a Late-Blooming Martyr	27
Auntie Star-of-the-Weekend	29
Clothes for the Naked	31

THREE

Il Fortuna	35
Acta Gratuita	37
Conversion Disorder	39
Brief History with Christianity	41

FOUR

The Road to the Cathouse Is Paved with Sharp Scissors	45
Is He Floating?	48

Flor de Tabacos	50
Edward	51
All of a Tin Stove without Heat	52

FIVE

Oh Prosthetic	57
Any Small Cake or Cookie	59
Details from the Southeast Quadrant	62
Attar of Roses	64

SIX

How Many Times Have You Been a White Swan?	69
Catfish	71
Palimpsest of Barefoot Doctors	72
Theory of Celestial Navigation	75
On Refusing Poison	77
You Big Monster You	79

ONE

Silky Turnpike

We never show up dead, now do we?
And who always does the driving?

You don't have to shout in front
of the children, sighs my mother,
looking at the buildings passing
by. My brother in his diaper is
wedged in between them.

I sit in the backseat on my knees,
arms around my father's neck.
He's a lemon-scented cigarette.
When I grow up, I'll be your
girlfriend.

My mother pulls my sleepy brother
to her lap. Her lips grow thin.

You're just too old to talk like that
and you're much too big for dolls.

Someday I'll be forty-seven.
I better pull myself together.
I think I need a husband or two.

We'll take a safari to honeymoon,
sit in the lap of a World War jeep,
lurch through dry, yellow scrub
and twisted trees.

My husband, pale counter, he's
sitting beside me, and la, his bony
hand is on my knee. Poor darling

isn't doing well. Let's cut this short
then. I can afford it. We'll sail across
one brief sea, float home in trains.

I take it all back with me. Bonjour,
New Jersey, you fat doll's arm.

Beautiful Women Are Easy on the Eye

Years ago that was how they billed
Hawaii: a haven of grass-skirted
beauties, arms waving, all waiting
for pale New Jersey.

My father in his Bermuda shorts
must have whistled loud coming
down from the twin-engine plane.
*Bejesus, it's hot. It's pretty darn
hot for paradise. Whew.*

The native girls look nearly
naked on the postcard he sent:

I ate a real roast pig, he wrote.
*You should have seen it. All
covered in banana leaves and sweet.*
They light torches wherever he goes.

Fabulous, says my mother, lips
barely moving. My sister sings
Aloha Oe in the driveway.

What she wouldn't give for
a real ukulele. My mother looks
out and sees those chubby arms,
tells me: *Your father's whooping
it up in the islands right now.*

We are all learning a secret hula
for when he comes back: *arms like
this and pretty.*

Living in and alongside Prowlers

The man in the moon stood
with one foot on a fallen
tree. *That's no bachelor,*
my mother said. It was my
father. The picnic basket
swung from his long arms.

But it wasn't my father
when we snuck up closer.
The plaid pants were all
wrong. We bundled up in
the cold and hurried on.

The man with a basket ran
after us, but we flew like
antimatter. *That's just
like a thinker,* my mother
told me. And he was gone.

We stopped at a farm, where
a man pulled weeds up with
his hands. *That's your true
father,* my mother whispered;

he's a farmer. She brushed
the dirt from the hem of my
coat and fixed my hair with
five red roses. We shouted,

waved hello; at one point
I became a constellation.
But who can see a star by
day? We waited for ages;
the sun would not go down.

I looked nothing like him
with his pale green skin.
Recessive genes, my mother
murmured; *people walk all
over him, naming the weeds.*

Loveladies, New Jersey

My baby brother wears my old
bikini bottoms at the beach,
digs up sand crabs by the handful,

but he can barely catch them
in his fat-folded fingers.

He asks me about the orange crud
in one crab. I tell him it's eggs.

He drops the orange one gently,
calling it *Aunt Vivvy*, who's
pregnant and might burst open.

I'm rising up and then falling
with the ocean; my brother is
back in the white white sand.
I tell myself he's collecting shells.

My skinny mother waves me in;
she's doubled over laughing,
tells my brother, *don't move.*

I ask, why do I have to get out?
She says, *go look at your brother.*

He is sitting on the towel, tapping
the cooler. Each fat finger is stuck
inside a pink plastic tampon shell.

I look at my mother in her nothing
bikini and make him take them off.

Floating like Plums

One summer, three uncles
floated away. First went
the uncle who jumped in
his trunks every morning.

He was a young father,
brown and pleasing,
dragged around a jetty
one morning by a strong
riptide.

His children watched him
wash up over rocks
like a bleeding seal,
arms too broken to swim.

A stranger ran miles
to drag him ashore.

Later that June, an uncle
went boating, and he did
not love his wife or son,
of this we're certain.

A storm flew in, shutting
the bay down and black.
The boat came back, all
emptied and floating.

In August, the fat uncle
fell overboard while
fishing for blue marlin.

His canvas shoes slipped
out from beneath him.
His pale green face flashed
like the moon on the water.

Two boys on board were
torn between horror and
shame: *your fat father
bobbing in the ocean.*

But also: *your father
stuck in blood water,*
marlin all but forgotten,
boat leaving him behind
before circling back,

four older men holding
the smaller boy down
by his thin wild limbs,
buckets of chum kicked
over in the scuffle.

The uncle thought briefly
of swimming it in,
but he was not the uncle
who threw a dog across
a room for something.

He was the gentle uncle,
ashamed to be crying, arms
white and soft in the sea.

Arms on Fire

Before I was a tinder in my father's eye,
I was a red firecracker in a black powder
shack in Malaysia. I slept for days after
the making of me, the rolling, tamping
down, the wrapping. I was raw, slightly
waxy, made in minutes and put aside.

My brother was tied to the foot of me, my
sister tied to my hair. We talked that way,
from string to string and back. Contrary
to all our expectations, we stayed put.

And then when we thought it was all about
staying put, we were taken out in thin boxes,

strung up on flagpoles and wrapped around
the temple eaves. Lanterns bobbed above us
like apples, persimmons, buttocks, cheeks,
and they kept their distance. No one spoke
to us. We talked along our threaded spine,
until someone cried, *I'm hot! I'm dying!*

I burst with a bang along the match-lit string.
The air shook with smoke and temple bells.
Bits of red paper settled over dogs and people.
Our heads hung down like dry, black fruits;
somehow that was the start of a new year.

When the monsoons came, we washed into
one of the muddy creeks, sucked past clumps
of yellow grass and bits of burnt-up string.

In the new world, fathers blinked like stars,
mothers beamed like red planets, we came

wrapped in flannel and did not remember
the holiday in Malaysia. This time it was hard
to pass along the sparks, we looked so strange:
all limbed and haired and full of warm water.

Still, we were on fire when the new year broke
open around us. Mother gave us pots and pans.
The streets grew loud with shouts and clanging.

My head was full of black gunpowder but I did
not sift into red tissue paper. My body refused
to go up in smoke.

The President-Maker

*I couldn't cut the bread into nice, thin
slices, so I ended up with a sandwich
as big as a dictionary. I was mortified*

*eating that sandwich. The other students
were right not to sit by me. I would hate
a boy who brought a sandwich like that
to school. I would hate him.*

Pardon me, that's not your president.
He's no prime minister; he never held
public office. Between you and me,
the man loathes dark suits.

But you've noticed he's wearing one.
You mistaking him for a head of state
speaks of your own good taste.
Do not beg to differ: he's no prince.

*I had to wear shoes with braces on them,
salmon-colored shoes with silver braces.
There was something wrong with my leg.*

He doesn't own a Purple Heart, nor think
of ways to bring water to the village.
The women would love him if he did so,
but he doesn't know this. He is bad
with numbers and worse with names.

I don't know what he does at his desk
all day, or where he goes for lunch.
Maybe he eats in the park, pushing crumbs
carefully to the edge of the bench.

I know he would have said a kind word,
would have shared his apple, but who
knew you were hungry? Did you mention
it in your conversation? You never once
volunteered any such information.

His trick knee troubles him sometimes.
He said to tell you he's always careful
walking along, ready to catch himself.
He says, thank you for asking about him.

How nice of you to notice my slight limp.

Next time, you should point out that you
are hungry, that you need an autograph,
that the apple looks nice in his hand.

But he is not a president, and now you
say you don't really want his lunch.
I'm confused. There are crumbs all over.

That is the trouble with homemade bread.

Trawl Line, Trawl Line, Sugarplum

It's late and I know he's either with another woman or he's dead.

Did you go to college? Did you take a degree? Yes. Yes to all that. Then he had to marry a summertime fling. *She was in a family way.*

He fathered three sticky barnacle daughters; we called them cousins and enjoyed their vacation house.

Their father was timber-limbed and handsome candy. One windy afternoon, he took his boat off the choppy shore, going fishing despite a storm.

My mother leans down for the story, kneels on a yellow towel. I'm taking a bath, plastic boats bobbing over my fat legs, a washcloth covering my private parts, my baby candy.

They found the boat in a nearby marina, no signs of life or soda cans, nothing caught in a trawler, such a mystery, says my mother.

We signal S.O.S., tap it out in a brief Morse code: A.l.l..t.h.e..u.n.c.l.e.s. .a.r.e..l.e.a.v.i.n.g..

It's like they never heard of New Jersey.

One night, a storm washes away part of
the backyard, flings beach grass up to
the porch. Fish, dead fish, give a last
shine to the welcome mat: *Come on in!*

The backyard is a bucktooth sticking
out in salt water.

Girl cousins sit in the living room.
The fringe on the sofa bottom is wet
with the water coming under the door.
They're waiting for him to wash in.

I draw my own bath and scream with
the hot water faucet I can't shut off.
Water thunders into the tub; boats fall
sideways over the unwinking drain.

Where is my mother, where is my mother?

She's doing a pineapple cha-cha in the
sewing room, asks me not to spill her
gin, not to fiddle with her cigarettes.

I ignore the stuck faucet running upstairs
filling the tub, the water spilling over
their tiles, leaking in between the walls.

Electric sockets spit blue fire first, then
lukewarm water. Parti-color plastic boats
float downstairs.

Girl cousins see this and nod: *it's a sign,*
they tell each other. It's a sign.

TWO

Tea-Stained, Vermilion

Her shoes on the wet asphalt
were steel needles ticking
through tightly woven fabric.

She was running to get some-
where, running right down
the middle of the road, more

solid yellow line than sensible
woman, more movie star than
"take to the hills!" Click, click.

She knew nothing about opium,
not even the poppy it came
from, but she was born in red

flowers. The nurses lost her
in the underbrush; they looked
for her with silver droppers.

Once she talked too much at
a party of men, even her dress
was just too much red, meaning

please, please pay attention,
meaning she wasn't listening.
Still, her hair was curled over

a hot glass pipe and her heels
were sharp as great pinpricks
in those sandals. That was so

long ago it seems like another
language. The letters are very
spindly, like rusty gazebos, and

inside the light is soft brown; it
comes through a teabag, I think.
To tell the truth, who knows what

happened? We lived in the saw-
tooth meadow; grasses snapped at
our waists and thighs. I think we

were running, someone was after
us—the usual dream. I had my
hands full of old, nasty flowers.

We threw them behind us, then
heard the clang clang of villains
running smack into iron. More

fairy tale than actual danger, still,
her face was all white poppies back
then; she'd been underfoot for ages.

Filters out Twigs and Sticks

A small coughing *khuh khuh khuh* inside the radio last night.

Coughing right through the opus. Tiny brutes. I heard the smallest nose, a nose like a pin drop, sniffle.

Radio influenza. Take precautions immediately. Air raids following. Opus ignored, *khuh khuh.*

Another air raid: roach drops out of folded napkin halfway to lips.

Drops and rolls across minted veal pomegranate. Exit table left.

Diner: Stunned! Repulsed! Close-up to lips all crumb-resplendent.

I could hear people coughing between the catgut strings of violins.

Is everybody playing sick? Also of interest: a girl who peeled back the skin of her arms, *oh razor.*

Not to worry, she said. All clear. *Just checking,* she said. Just checking for what the hell? I said.

Checking the substance of under her skin. She thought she might be worms underneath, but so far,

not yet. She is not a folded napkin
yet, she is not something sick inside

a radio yet. But there is coughing in
my brain soprano. And what might

crawl in my ear one night and get to
my thinking faster than I can type?

Plunge

Knives are dumb because
they don't know what to cut.
This is bread, that's my finger.
Lay off the finger.
Knives are dumb, you see.
They'll cut through anything
regardless of what you want sliced.

That lame steel arm falls all
over you if you're not careful.
Put a loaf underneath it
and nothing else. Watch for the
sides of your hands, those slender
hams: they're not for chopping.

Watch, too, for the tips of thumbs.
They go like sticky butter pats,
fall to the floor with a slap
like a mouse dropping
from a building out of fright.

Chances are good he'll dent your car
if he fell from a far enough height.
Somebody'll ask if you hit hail.
Oh no, it was a rodent.
He was plastered all over:
the bon vivant of his crowd.

Recall the girl on the Empire State
who went through the roof
of a yellow sedan.
She had a lot of velocity
by the time she struck.

Did some damage, lost a shoe.
She was settled like an angel,
arm poking crooked from her suit.

There's a falling that's lurching
from not being caught.
It's a dumb knife slicing,
a small mouse falling,
a swift whirling planet,
pulling girls from tops
of buildings when they step off.

The New Plutonium

Some faces cannot be labored for.
Either one is lovely or one is not.

Even in the worst of times, famines,
bread crusts always found their way
to her comely hand. Still, it was difficult.

Once she was cut up and made into
a thick blood pudding. Luckily,

her beauty was too good for just
one supper. Miraculously, she rose

from blood in the flour, her lips
like wine, as if never even eaten
by everyone present.

The wickedest cook slipped away to
the kitchen, flew to the great muddy
river, plunged under the pale flowers.

White lilies bring death to a kitchen.
They are an ill omen. Beware most
white blossoms. Never let untutored
florists tell you otherwise: all white
flowers mean evil by any stove.

A bitter cook in a flowery kingdom
is never benign. What is the nicest
pudding if you are sewn up inside it?

Watch the cooks. Watch what they put
in the stew pot.

Do not eat anything covered in white
petals, even when they tell you it
is something-something with chicken.

Flowers are easily recognizable in food.
Bitter cooks will sure and wreak havoc;
they have precious little to command.

Their magic bodes ill: *a pigeon heart
full of three hundred pins makes a man
marry you. Never let the soup stick.*

*That bitch upstairs. Bury the heart
by the light of the moon. Leave it.*

Sleep by the light of a moon and you will
go mad. Eventually, you go mad anyway,
but at least your skin will be bone china.

You cannot be too exquisite. The cooks
will still hate you with porcelain skin.

Gently, gently, drop the bird blood in
flour. You will bloom out of the mouths
that chew you.

Notes for a Late-Blooming Martyr

According to a Russian spy
satellite, all's well at Judy's
house. You needn't do her

dirty laundry or even keep
her company this evening.
You can wash your own hair,
O martyr.

Most women who try to kill
themselves eat sleeping pills.
They make miraculous come-
back patterns; they lie in bed

like wilted orchids, breathing.
If I know Judy, she doesn't
really want to die.

All you people teetering on
parapets, come back inside
the buildings, won't you?

Rust shut, oh guns, and dull
down, you knives. Bid adieu
to your splendid stigmata.

What if at the last minute
a soldier ran up to Jesus
on that red splintered cross,

saying he'd heard it on high,
it wasn't to be the fine son
of God after all, but a bunch

of burning white cattle. Two
herds were already on fire.
Jesus should come and see it.

Imagine the world intact,
and the universe, too, the
earth's crust lightly floating.

It makes you slightly ill
just thinking about it.

The sun, too, slings itself
around the galaxy. Funny
how we get giddy whirling.

I saw Saturn through an old
telescope. It was nothing but
a dot with a thin white pin

through it. How can anything
be so far away? Calling Judy.
Come in, Judy.

Auntie Star-of-the-Weekend

A lady in the kitchen is bent
over a black cookie sheet,
putting powder up her nose.

Tra lee! Tra lee! Tra lee!
I barely know who I'm sitting on.

Not a *who,* a what, a lawn chair.
I'm sitting on it, arms out stiff
like a man at his paper taking
in the news of the world, but
barely and at a length from himself:

So and So's Armored Car
A Terrible Explosion
Influx of Poisonous Bees

Luckily, all I see are trees
putting forth miniature leaves;
aspen, maple, sycamore, oak.
A yew bush will cover flaws.

The woman in the kitchen sees
much more than is good for her.

She will throw herself over
any old, steep bank, landing
in brambles to scratch up
her point. None of us watch

her scream through the rooms,
loosing small, personal gestures
only friends would know. Tics
and jerks pass over like comets.

We miss most of what she does.
Today she's all of humanity;
someday she'll be a kind, old
aunt, her purse full of dollars.

She will let you drive her long
blue car through floodwaters,
will send a dress your mother
finds vulgar. It will be red.

Mum in the bathroom, her mouth
full of pins, looks you over
and over with a cold sharp eye.
Her lips go thin then thinner.

She pulls the dress together
across your bosom, wonders
what your aunt was thinking.
Pulls the dress again as if
to make your breasts go away.

Your aunt would look at you
and say *you're filling out*.
She'd be delighted, a wind-
chime in her mouth about it,

as if that's what she hoped
you'd do: wake up one morning
in spring and flesh your ribs
out to please her.

Clothes for the Naked

Knit mittens for the weary, succor the lonely, that sort of thing...

God certainly loves girls not quite inside the line called pure. Newly-driven slush, I'd call them, not too far fallen. They get all the glory.

Imagine whatever's slightly smutty about them: a memory of fine silk stockings, a pumice stone, a naked foot in someone's lap. Unsavory; still, we read on.

I'm not making fun, *I'm not making fun at all*. I'd chop my heels off to fit inside, cut my two thumbs down, whittle my good leather shoes to a black set of neck chokers.

I might have become one Poor Clare, sugar-curing bacon for the naked, clothing the softly folding flesh of men. I would have let them in

like fatted calves, would have put the gold upon them. But there is something lousy about me: charity never slid out of my hands nicely.

I was once a heavy, plain-faced bride, dollar bills pinned to a yellowy veil. We cashed in on the money dance.

I remember somebody fixed me
for the picture, plumped up my
starch-stiff train, told the wind:
don't blow.

My husband, thin twin, was nervous
at my side. There's no smile in my
square face, none at all. I must have
made a secret sign: *pass by, carry on.*

The guests said that we'd never make
it, that I'd force you into dust and you
would take it. I married you because

no one would have me: who could
be bothered to make me bad? And
so you took me, the fatted virgin,
a girl, an innocent, an angry bride.

THREE

Il Fortuna

Pardon, is this the last box?
The last box at the opera?

Then I should take it.
See how it suits me?
Crushed velvet?
I like it.
Ditto the chandelier.

Send the waiter up
with three gold cups
for water.
Let the spring
beneath my chair
bubble up and over.

The chorus is humming far below
and I know the tune
it signifies.
Next comes the woman
with mutilated eyes.

She popped them out
with two gold thumbs.
It's part of the tragedy.
That's why the dancers
look a little wilted:
they're emoting.

All you with your eyes covered,
your ears half-cocked
for screams:
you can come out now.
She's met the man of her dreams

and he doesn't mind
her braille cue cards.

We all breathe a sigh
from the reef
and ready ourselves for
the last act,
the *lastadella*
of books and other props,
the act full of cellos.

In lieu of talking
back and forth,
you hear bows-on-strings.

And all this time our
conductor is crying.
He's so in love
his flutes are straining.

Cymbals clack together
with a shudder:
this denotes flooding.

People pour out into the aisles
like minnows or krill.
I crumble bread over
their silver shoulders.
Take this, I whisper. *Shove over.*

Acta Gratuita

St. Patrick drove the snakes from Ireland,
and what am I doing this morning? Lying
like a bean in the middle of my bed.

Francis Xavier the Confessor walked
the streets, ringing a bell for children
and slaves, calling them to catechism.

He called out, *Candy! Candy for you!*
And to some it was candy and to others
it was more bitter. I do not have his

fire. Act the saint, and soon you might
become one. Is that what you desire?
I should give the bed away, the blankets,

too. I lie here thinking about it. I ring
bells and call the servants to me. *Paper!*
Something to write with! They stumble.

I scream in the red one's face. *Paper!*
And pen! The pen is necessary! Ink!
Truthfully, I get up. There is no maid

waiting. *Paper, where are you?* I take
it from its special drawer, sit it down.
Paper, learn your place. I just might

rip you to pieces for reasons your thin
head will never decipher. Oh Pen, give
me your firstborn son. Put his head

*on the rock and poke it. Poke him again.
Put a snake in his mouth. Do all this
because you love me. Take him home.*

*Tell him all about me. Paper, sit your
daughter on a match. Burn her.* I will!
I will! I'll explain it all later.

Conversion Disorder

I

Brave Saint Brigid gave a leper
water, the water turned to
milk, and lo,

spots fell from the leper's
skin, fingers reattached
themselves from where
they'd lately fallen.

It was a miracle, a scream,
a yell. A sick person drank
tepid water and got well.

II

Blessed Gertrude, though a
virgin, had a calling, found
her breasts swollen with milk.

For months she nursed the
savior, which was helpful.

As well she received all five
stigmata—*hands, feet, heart,
shoulders, head*—bled cherry-
colored water on Mondays.

III

Saint Margaret of Hungary
embarrassed her maid,
threw herself fiercely
face down in the mud
for God's love. And sure

did her maid find this
revolting and told her
so, which only left muddy
Saint Margaret beatific.

IV

Saint Juliana, stubborn
mule, she was beheaded.

V

Saint Agnes was denounced
as a Christian; justice
sentenced her to a brothel.

It is said she retained
her virginity only through
miraculous intervention.
It must have been something.

VI

Saint Milburga against her
better wishes put her heavy
hands all over a dying boy's

body, thus recalled the fire
which held the thin spirit
fast by the tail. She forced
the tiny, bluish baby shell
to an encore convulsion.

His milky lungs filled up
like cups; his eyes went
wild with trying. A sick
child not expected to live,
he was a second time in dying.

Brief History with Christianity

Imagine forty-four years absorbed in prayer under a tree that bloomed at last and in the middle of a dead winter. They built a monastery by the unreasonable flowers.

Why put the praying one under an eight-hundred-pound weight? Who could have survived it?

And the iron hooks? The vinegar bath? The salt, the fetters, plus the filthy pen of wild beasts that did not touch the one in prayer, just trembled and kept to one side?

All at once there were loathsome diseases, locusts came, and other vermin. The people wondered if anyone was elated anywhere in the world. No one answered them.

They looted their own houses, left outside their best clothes, hoped their belongings would be stolen while planking the bier for one who was hunchbacked and dainty.

During the seasons, the martyrs wove sonnets, braided sandals, demonstrated means of absorbing disdain with radiant tree-flowers.

Soon, they kept saying, very soon
a child will rise up over this pasture
and flatbread will bake in the hot
mouths of beasts. Remove each loaf
with a tender caution; give all
to the lepers. Write about it.

FOUR

The Road to the Cathouse Is Paved with Sharp Scissors

It was forbidden for the church
to shed blood: blades were unholy.
Heretics were strangled or burnt.

Drowning was only an option for
lake or riverside congregations
and the choir by the sea.

Ladies of certain medieval evenings
found themselves chained together
underwater, screaming, clawing

each other, face powder rising
to the surface in gusts. Such
was their pre-Renaissance glory.

The apples of Sodom turn to ashes
on the lips. That is all the good
knowledge you get from them.

Take the apples and cut them up,
why don't you? A pair of scissors
is only two knife blades joined

together at the pivot point.
Pinking shears have sawtooth
edges which prevent fabric from

unraveling. The bridge from this
world to the next is thinner than
that thread, thinner than a scissor

edge, and hard to walk over. The
whole notion is manifestly absurd.
How to explain the mess I've made

of myself? My crisscrossed skin?
Start with the Marvel-of-Peru.
Keep talking. Flowers to fauna,

fauna to rocks, rocks to sand, then
sand into glass, which when broken
becomes shards. That's plenty sharp

enough to do some damage, create
a furor. Keep your wrists at
arm's length; do not be tempted

to open yourself up. Your blood
is not the ocean, has no business
swimming from you; put the glass

down and quit drinking. I've got
a much better idea. Why don't
you wear the stockings while *I*

take the pictures? You can keep
the film, I don't care. It won't
cost you a penny extra.

Now say, *Hi, I'm Sandy.* That's
perfect. Now I want you to spread
your legs a little, scissor them

and lean over. Hold your hands
up to catch the doves coming in
through the window. I know you

don't know what time it is. This
room is an undone thread and you
walk along the precipice, shouting

Cocktails! Cocktails, everyone!
Welcome to the cabaret. The man
at the gate is presently tied up

in stockings. He will cut himself
out and swim to the top of the tank
in under a minute. Somebody time him.

Is He Floating?

Why talk about the devil at all? He's
filled with bitterness as anybody is.
He's a larva nothing, a rusted crabtrap,

a jimmy with his claws gone, a softshell
influenza. Remember how the sourness
inside us floods up and then recedes?

Devils, too, sometimes crack up or dry out
and swim for shore because it's too much,

even for those born to it. Think of him,
a red mermaid, his tail limp as a scarlet
stocking, his horns white with drying salt.

Candy man, red twist, who knew what to do
with you? I was plankton in those days,
but not entirely useless, somewhat motile.

In the water, I'm food, sometimes coloring,
as in *red tide*. I'm beautiful but stupid.
I had no idea what I was swirling around.

What is a boardwalk? Who put casinos in
the water? Why did ladies throw pennies?

Who ate the people every night and spit
them out the next morning looking more
and more haggard? Looking, indeed, as if

they had a message for the rest of us but
had forgotten what it was. *Come on with
the two horse!* some of them screamed,

but I had no idea where they kept their
mounts. The three cherries never lined
up and gave a fortune. I would have put
my money in, but I was plankton, remember.

People yelled themselves hoarse at each
other the closer they came to winning
then fell silent. I wanted this to end

with all the guests leaping like new fish
in the water, but I couldn't get them to
listen. I had no vocal cords; the English

language was something strange to me.
It was nothing to me, to be perfectly
honest. I knew piers, stilts, water,

water, pieces of salt—oh was I small.
I saw everything and then something
made me open up and eat it. I never

even thought to myself, *am I hungry?*
I just slipped forward and took it.

It was either good or not good: who can
tell? I was motile but not aesthetic.
It was crimson, a bit of tail, oh god

but it was bitter, bitter like vinegar,
only I have no idea what vinegar is and
it would hurt me to actually drink it.

Flor de Tabacos

I leave a light on so you won't fall down,
but the bulb bleats all night long.

Only the eyes hear the small bright cries,
and sleep is hard to climb into.

I jerk awake in a thousand bee dances;
big lot of flowers at ninety fourteen—
a pecan limb falling, one missed step,

blooms full of pollen, left, right, left.
You fumble into bed, smoke and clothes.

Guitar picks fall like teeth from your
pockets and all the sleepy tulips
slip up from the sheets.
Our nest is coming somewhat undone.

My chest is full of wet hornets; cigarettes
live in your hair.
They keep falling and laughing
from the sheets in between us.

Not clean, they whisper, *not clean.*

My feet cannot stay still; they kick
a horizontal rumba just under our
blanket. It's a tricky wool stepping;

now I'm treading flowered water.
Sweaters in the closet tremble,
books in the kitchen fall down.

Edward

The butchers knew a thing or
two, but they weren't talking,
just sawing away at another
old carcass. You were all wrong

about my teeth looking like
ten lemondrops, but I stopped
smiling. I let my lips cool.

I knew you like the flywheel
or carburetor, which is to say
I had no idea where to find you.

But I do know how you sound,
your voice clipped like tin.
Everything since is guttural

or too long in the speaking
of. Anyway. Where have I been
this whole time? Smiling like

a new mezzaluna? Steel shanks
falling from under my tongue?
What do you serve with that?

What has an underbite of melons
and brine, smoothness from oak?
Pardon, I mean *ache*. That's where

this loudness springs from. Now
nothing tastes like cigarettes,
and I know for a fact he smokes.

All of a Tin Stove without Heat

Because there aren't chunks
of land on that planet,
storms gather momentum
and linger for ages, like you
and I in our last weeks,

wet, angry, and red,
feet floating somewhere
at the end of the bed,

our heads like two white
dwarves and screaming.
I heard the red spot
on Jupiter is a hurricane.

The ring around Saturn
is bits of an old moon
that came too close
and imploded.

In your apartment, the dust
finds the left-behind
parts of me, the guest soaps
of me, my old shampoo.

Still, my heart will not
explode or peter out.
That one storm on Jupiter
is longer than all of us;

our lives arc beneath it,
two weak electric threads.

We fall through it all
like two red plums,
four hands out to catch us—
throats tight when we don't.

FIVE

Oh Prosthetic

Geometry, the hexagon, all of it
a triangle and a clatter of chalk.
Our teacher had a manmade arm,
beige pink and simple-shaped.

He tucked it under his other arm,
the arm with the hand that held
the broken white chalk.

But always on a radius or parallel
line, that rubber arm would slip
its cover, flop down, and flail,

a rock in a stocking, until caught
up again by the chalk-bearing hand,
stern parent that it must have been.

We were silent behind him, watched
the arcs of the circumference with
great care. The man at the board
never said a word outside of formulas

and areas defined. Not even when
we snickered would he whirl around
to find us suddenly slack-faced,

as if our chins did not quiver with
the heft of those bland fingers.

I knew a fellow who lost a finger
climbing down from an old camp truck.

Somehow he caught his wedding ring
on a hook. When the truck took off,
he was left behind screaming, finger
collared to the side, stuck in a last
come hither.

🌸

It isn't that we don't truly love
pin-straight legs or the long bending
arms of stars,

but that we can make do without them,
tell ourselves, *these are not the only
things that fall away or leave us.*

Still, it's awful, the unexpected exit,
a bon voyage to finger, hand, or thigh.

Any Small Cake or Cookie

Imagine newfound galaxies
aligned like spoons
laid out for tea.

The sugar in its sugar lumps
an afternoon spread out
like stars.
Neighbors falling into
each other's arms.

How do you do?
to all new planets
who might well hold
hordes of other oceans
that brew their own kinds
of fish.

Press your best dress;
put the kettle on.
Call the cat.
Call the cat, will you;
get her sitting pretty.
We might have company.

Hello, many planets
and all those stars
who flew like quail
from the first black hole:

a trailer full of massive bodies
making dinner,
cooking moons,
picking rocks from beans.

Then all at once flinging back
the old screen door,
everybody running swiftly,
ripping through the windows

to hurtle off fast. What?
Is father drunk again?
Loutish planet.

No matter. For some reason,
they've scattered.
I'll miss you
whispers through the universe.

My sister the physicist
will understand
the edgy galaxy,
may explain exactly why
it flew apart.
All the same, her cat must
be let out and bees avoided.

I broke her arm in two
neat halves ages ago,
and still
there's a pinch
in my stomach.

I wouldn't like to be fingered
or even called to the rug
about it.

I don't wish to be found wanting.

Let me be better than
the rest of the ship
all slightly greedy
and myopic.

Will they snicker over several
who say they've been taken
aboard alien boats,
had their private parts examined,
and returned?

Mainly what I want to say is:
be gentle with every
limb: they're fragile.
Take splints to the people
who need them.
Do not sit at home all day:
the world is so lonely without you.

A shining future is predicted,
full of starlit guests pocketing
hors d'oeuvres to study later.
Put them at ease.
Have your daughter offer
cups and cups of tea.

They may well pick through us
like fat summer peas,
pulling the good from the shriveled
or crippled at heart.

They may wish
we were better than we are.
No matter: smile, pour.

Details from the Southeast Quadrant

I understand now, the officers' wives
taking tea during battles. Nibbling
what you wouldn't call a biscuit at
any time other than war. Sometimes
there was sugar; often there was not.

Always they did without something,
discussed it amongst themselves,
hoped that soon this would be over.

A soldier leaning against his pack
enjoys an after-dinner cigarette.
He is very young yet. I have no idea
what he's seen or where he's sore.

There are plenty of opportunities
to lead a lonely life. Somebody's
husband may never come home, may
come home changed. A man might lose
every friend and come home without
much of himself inside his own skin.

A woman might sit and have tea with
three widows. None of them mind
discussing just sugar. The soldier
sends a wreath of smoke into the air.

Somebody sitting up at night should
not be smoking, should not make
a target of himself. But dinner
was finished and it was that time.

I will tell you how it is: the sun
sinks down, dinner is eaten, every
body is a planet. We turn and face
the end of the day in our particular
fashion: with tea or smoke, oyster
forks, sugar tongs and linen napkins.

Attar of Roses

He was shedding red flowers with every
exhale. The bed spilled bent tulips
over everyone's shoes.

He told his family he was ungodly tired:
can't they lean closer? In a whisper,
he said, *I don't like to shout: it startles
the horses who have nowhere to go.*

He had two scarlet barns out back by
a stand of hackberry trees. It was Kentucky.

Birds ate the small, hard fruits. We
were covered in red flowers. From under
the covers came a ripe, hothouse smell.
He might have been on fire, briefly.

Who wasn't tired when the rain finally
came? Why did he ask us to come closer?

The birds were full of berries. We were
quiet, waiting for the water, catching
his words, but barely. He was so lovely,

we didn't like to disturb him, but we
had to undo him. Who followed the
red flowers from his collar to the hole
in his throat where they fell from?

One of us, one of us did. Funny how
I don't remember who discovered this.

And someone sewed him up like a good
wool coat; then he was strong again.
He sat up in bed and looked us over.
Flowers sifted to the bedroom floor.

By the morning he was busy near one of
the two barns. We watched him walk back
and forth between the hackberry trees.
He'd looped a rope over his left arm.

At the edge of the meadow, blue spruce
perched like pigeons, gray and fragrant,
needles for beaks. It was raining out.

What did he just say? We lean forward.

The things I keep trying to tell you.

SIX

How Many Times Have You Been a White Swan?

Our uncle upstairs is practically dead.
The aunts know what to do with him:
wrap the sheet up, point the foot of

the bed toward the door, wail loudly.
They are tying him up against leakage.
A coffin is hammered together out back.

That's the third batch of white flowers
today. Send him up the Hudson River,
that long, gray strip of aching water,

with flowered banks and ice in cracks.
Everyone's busy giving orders although
he's not dead yet. But we keep hoping.

Not that we want anyone ill or lonely,
but nobody is getting married anytime
soon, and no one will understand that
the empire waist followed the course
of the last empire.

Hems go up and up until you're afraid
to look, but you will look, you will hear
hammering out back and hope it's just
a cane chair, but who'd take a hammer

to that? An aunt puts jade in his mouth,
keeps him from leaving a restless soul, but
he is not a gone flicker yet, there's breath

pooled at the back of the spine and head.
It's just begun swimming from the mouth
of his body, swims through the wet bowls

of milk on the dresser, set out to appease
a vampire god. But he is not a gypsy,
nor will he haunt even as much as a dog.

The sweetish-smelling body isn't moving;
several aunts are wailing and touching
the edge of that bed. He would so love

to be under their hands one last time,
would love to be in the two still pools
of blood behind the spine, but no. Now

it's a pinched-up shoe, and his foot
won't go where he'd like it to, cannot
put itself back from where it's left off

dying. The milk bowls and the aunts swim
softly in the distance on their feathers.
The hammering out back will finally stop.

Catfish

*A mouth like a split foot, each
whisker a twitching gray stick.*

The lily pads were silver hub-
caps in black water; the light

from the library cast everything
pencil-colored and starry. Hard

to call anything green. Scents
were sharp: the twigs, trees,
the heavy oil under the leaves.

I might have been loosed bread,
minnows taking small, fast bites
before continuing as before.

Such is their wet lot, as ours
is breathing, eating, talking
about ourselves to each other.

The important thing is to stay
wriggling. The moving is good.

The trees bent low around us;
the sky fell into scarves. Stars

waited like pins behind the air.
Something underwater was ravenous.

Palimpsest of Barefoot Doctors

Medicine is truly splendid but hardly
keeps us from falling in harm's way.
We're always stumbling all over each

other, breaking every limb and bone
inside us, even the little ones in
our ears. No wonder we step around

thin cracks in the pavement, motion
black cats out of our path. We may
feel foolish doing so, but that won't

stop us. Think of Aunt Pity who lived
on the liquid hanging in bags which
withered her down to a listless white

heron. They did not bleed her, nor
ply her with leeches, nor did anyone
ask us just *who* might have cursed her.

The old way of magic, the dirty wand,
spitting in the sick one's face,
is just that: old. No longer truly

necessary, no longer calling on blue-
black smoke. Now they're dispensing
chalky penicillin; well, it's a spell,

too. Take one rye loaf of rotten
bread, wait for the soft, shy patches
of gray-green and white, scrape six

black spots. Use to cool the inflamed
body, ease the swimming head, revive
what's delightful inside us. Despite

that, the people may not love Ludmila.
Her translated name means: tribe, grace,
favor, love. You know the supposed death-

ray inventor died of pancreatic cancer?
Oh, he's just like the rest of us who
go bad in our own ways. Forget the tools,

inventions, charms, chants, and curses.
For the record, it's possible the blue
Hope diamond is the emptied-out eye

of an idol from a temple in Burma. So,
where's the twin sister of the winking
blue stone? Which curse does she carry?

Could either sister forget her curse
and compare adventures? *I've been under
fabulous lock and key in a brick museum;*

everyone comes to see me. Yourself?
Well, the one sister, the one buried
in the earthquake, or by the monsoon,

or lost in terrible raids, she isn't
living in a lady's fancy necklace,
but she does know all the tricks.

She knows the way to arrange her hair,
her words, her limbs on satin pillows.
She's been blue in the face forever.

Bianca or Blanche may turn out swarthy.
Bernadette, despite her name, might not
have the resolution of a bear.

She may not be like her patron saint,
may never discover any healing waters.
She might be afraid to swim. Abigail,

should you so call her, may never be
a source of joy. Barbara, in ancient
Greek, means literally, *stammering*.

But aren't there Barbaras who become
both eloquent and familiar? Who can
say if Faith or Hope will wait nicely?

And Maristella, standing by the water
late at night, may never rise up full
of grace and shine. She may be frumpy,

a plain-faced girl, not normally given
to brilliant comments or patent leather.
Still, in her heart, she'll tell herself,

I'm a shining star, an asteroid, a comet.
Fishermen who look up and notice, knot
themselves more tightly to their lookout

chairs, whisper what they can to the slim
shoals of fish, wear the oily sweaters
their wives knit. They each whistle one

lucky tune, keep their ankles uncrossed,
name the boat with a chant on the water;
six nods to the miles of nothing below.

Theory of Celestial Navigation

The old parlor floor was a lady's cake, the dark wood black as Barcelona chocolate in the half light and strewn white with dust.

The almanac on the coffee table could not be opened to a wrong page. Every sentence depicted necessary altitude or heavenly bodies; each declination formed

a flower. The tea-takers grew girlish again, each drawing one fine foot across the sugared floor in measured, deliberate arcs.

Sandwiches sat in perfect angles; the tea tasted like flowers all afternoon; even the meat was lacy.

You were a girl in a fresh apron, waiting for daffodils and tulips to burst up out of your yard.

It happened last year, you said. All the lawn fell back in awe; red tulips waved you back and forth in and out of the house.

We had no idea how a tulip came up. Would it scream? Could you squeeze it? Did you wake up one night and look out over your starry,

black yard? Was the grass parting
like a smile? The tulips were tea
cups, weren't they? There were stars
in their water, in their black cups.

What was all that crashing? The new
blooms clattered like dishes in wind.
It was a racket. The daffodils turned
into spinsters, soft and falling open
so, so we ate them, green limbs and all.

On Refusing Poison

It's true, isn't it? A fly
midway between your ceiling
and the tiled floor is dying?

Despite flying with a vigor,
his days are numbered; he's
encumbered with the tiniest
red heart that cannot keep

to its metronome's ticking,
not indefinitely, anyway.

It was impossible to catch
him. I tried everything,
even the discarded cottage

cheese container trick, gaps
poked into the bottom so the
push of the wind would pass
right through that breakfast

vessel. Nonetheless, the fly
passed by for another window.
He was sinking. White tires

on a car mean someone's taking
a bride someplace, and someone
else is just about to marry her.

She's rising like a raisin in
yeast-made bread. There are
streamers, flowers, and sweet

cakes beneath her, plumping up
her dress, lifting her into
a chalky-wheeled car. Flowers

on a friend's white porch mean
he's dying, sinking through our
dreams like an alarm clock bell,
waking us with a vague unease,

as if we left something running
all night. Is the oven on? Did
the washer run gallons? No, that
was his heart again, ticking its

slow note, running like a motor
on the fumes we bring it: mint
plants, lilies, redbud blooms,

roses, daisies, oily, sweet candles.
Do not subside, oh lungs, brain, or
heart. Black fly, if only I could

put you out and let the wind lift
you, put the *tick, tick, tick* back
in your memory of things to do.

You Big Monster You

When she sat up, the mint-
green material fell
forward and into her lap.
She apologized through stitched-
together lips.

Oh those burial gowns:
what's a girl to do?

The undertaker was mortified,
the mourners, amazed.

The deceased holds her breasts
to cover them.
Hopping out of the casket,
she nearly falls.

She's a wildebeest.
Nobody touches her.
She's a charm.
They get quite close.

The back of her head is
parted neatly. She is
missing a few organs,
but walking.
You would call that
walking.
You would call that an
arm pushing the door
marked *Exit*.

She drifts through the
parking lot, past the cars

lined up.
She thinks to herself:
*I better get my mouth
back open.*

She better put on some decent
clothes. *God,* she thought,
What have I done now?